SWAMI VIVEKANANDA

BIOGRAPHY OF A GREAT THINKER, PHILOSOPHER AND MONK

INFO EDGE

Dedicated to Swami Vivekananda

A tribute from Info Edge Publications

Contents

Preface *vii*

1. Early Life 1
2. Education 3
3. Voyages Of Swami 11
4. Back In India 18
5. Nirvana 21
6. Philosophy 22

Preface

Master Vivekananda (12 January 1863 - 4 July 1902), conceived Narendranath Datta, was an Indian Hindu priest, scholar, and creator. He was a main devotee of the nineteenth-century Indian spiritualist Ramakrishna.[4][5] Influenced by Western esotericism,[6][7][8] he was a vital figure in the presentation of the Indian darsanas (lessons, rehearses) of Vedanta and Yoga to the Western world,[9][10][11] and is credited with raising interfaith mindfulness, carrying Hinduism to the situation with a significant world religion during the late nineteenth century.[12] He was a significant power in the contemporary Hindu change developments in India and added to the idea of patriotism in frontier India.[13] Vivekananda established the Ramakrishna Math and the Ramakrishna Mission.[10] He is maybe most popular for his discourse which started with the words "Siblings of America ...,"[14] in which he presented Hinduism at the Parliament of the World's Religions in Chicago in 1893.

Naturally introduced to a highborn Bengali Kayastha group of Calcutta, Vivekananda was leaned towards otherworldliness. He was impacted by his master, Ramakrishna, from whom he discovered that all living creatures were an encapsulation of the heavenly self; in this manner, administration to God could be delivered by the administration to mankind. After Ramakrishna's passing, Vivekananda visited the Indian subcontinent widely and gained direct information on the circumstances of winning in British India. He later went to the United States, addressing India at the 1893 Parliament of the World's Religions. Vivekananda directed many public and confidential talks and classes, scattering principles of the Hindu way of thinking in the United States, England, and Europe. In India, Vivekananda is viewed as an energetic holy person, and his birthday is praised as National Youth Day.[15][16]

CHAPTER ONE

Early Life

Vivekananda was conceived Narendranath Datta (abbreviated to Narendra or Naren)[18] in a Bengali family[19][20] at his genealogical home at 3 Gourmohan Mukherjee Street in Calcutta,[21] the capital of British India, on 12 January 1863 during the Makar Sankranti festival.[22] He had a place with a customary family and was one of nine siblings.[23] His dad, Vishwanath Datta, was a lawyer at the Calcutta High Court.[19][24] Durgacharan Datta, Narendra's granddad was a Sanskrit and Persian scholar[25] who left his family and turned into a priest at age twenty-five.[26] His mom, Bhubaneswari Devi, was a sincere housewife.[25] The moderate, normal disposition of Narendra's dad and the strict demeanor of his mom helped shape his reasoning and personality.[27][28] Narendranath was keen on otherworldliness from early on and used to reflect on the pictures of gods like Shiva, Rama, Sita, and Mahavir Hanuman.[29] He was captivated by meandering religious zealots and monks.[28] Narendra was mischievous and fretful as a youngster, and his folks frequently experienced issues controlling him. His mom said, "I petitioned Shiva for a child and he has sent me one of his demons".[26]

CHAPTER TWO

Education

In 1871, at eight years old, Narendranath enlisted at Ishwar Chandra Vidyasagar's Metropolitan Institution, where he went to class until his family moved to Raipur in 1877.[30] In 1879, after his family's re-visitation to Calcutta, he was the main understudy to get first-division marks in the Presidency College placement test. [31] He was an enthusiastic peruser of a wide scope of subjects, including reasoning, religion, history, sociology, workmanship, and literature.[32] He was likewise keen on Hindu sacred writings, including the Vedas, the Upanishads, the Bhagavad Gita, the Ramayana, the Mahabharata, and the Puranas. Narendra was prepared in Indian traditional music,[33] and consistently took part in actual activity, sports, and coordinated exercises. Narendra concentrated on the Western rationale, a Western way of thinking, and European history at the General Assembly's Institution (presently known as the Scottish Church College).[34] In 1881, he breezed through the Fine Arts assessment and finished a Bachelor of Arts degree in 1884.[35][36] Narendra concentrated on crafted by David Hume, Immanuel Kant, Johann Gottlieb Fichte, Baruch Spinoza, Georg W. F. Hegel, Arthur Schopenhauer, Auguste Comte, John Stuart Mill and Charles Darwin.[37][38] He became interested in the evolutionism of Herbert Spencer and related with him,[39][40] deciphering Herbert Spencer's book Education (1861) into Bengali.[41] While concentrating on Western savants, he likewise scholarly Sanskrit sacred texts and Bengali literature.[38]

William Hastie (head of Christian College, Calcutta, from where Narendra graduated) stated, "Narendra is a virtuoso. I have gone all over however I have never gone over a fellow of his gifts and conceivable outcomes, even in German colleges, among philosophical understudies. He will undoubtedly transform life".[42]

Narendra was known for his enormous memory and the capacity at speed perusing. A few episodes have been given as specific illustrations. In a discussion, he once cited word for word, a few pages from Pickwick Papers. One more occurrence that is given is his contention with the Swedish public where he gave reference to certain subtleties on Swedish history that the Swede initially contradicted but later surrendered. In one more occurrence with Dr. Paul Deussen at Kiel in Germany, Vivekananda was going over some poetical work and didn't answer when the teacher addressed him. Afterward, he was sorry to Dr. Deussen making sense that he was too caught up in perusing and thus didn't hear him. The teacher was not happy with this clarification, but rather Vivekananda cited and deciphered sections from the text, leaving the teacher astounded about his accomplishment of memory. Once, he mentioned a few books composed by Sir John Lubbock from a library and returned them the exceptionally following day, guaranteeing that he had understood them. The administrator wouldn't accept that him until questioning about the items persuaded him that Vivekananda was being truthful.[43]

A few records have considered Narendra a shrutidhara (an individual with an enormous memory).[44]

In 1880 Narendra joined Keshab Chandra Sen's Nava Vidhan, which was laid out by Sen in the wake of meeting Ramakrishna and reconverting from Christianity to Hinduism.[45] Narendra turned into an individual from a Freemasonry stop "eventually before 1884"[46] and of the Sadharan Brahmo Samaj in his twenties, a breakaway group of the Brahmo Samaj drove by Keshab Chandra Sen and Debendranath Tagore.[45][34][47][48] From 1881 to 1884, he was likewise dynamic in Sen's Band of Hope, which attempted to deter young people from smoking and drinking.[45]

It was in this cultic[49] milieu that Narendra got to know Western esotericism.[50] His underlying convictions were molded by Brahmo's ideas, which upbraids polytheism and the rank restriction,[29][51] and a "smoothed out, supported, monotheistic philosophy firmly hued by a particular and futuristic perusing of the Upanisads and the Vedanta."[52] Rammohan Roy, the organizer behind the Brahmo Samaj who was unequivocally impacted by unitarianism, endeavored towards a universalistic understanding of Hinduism.[52] His thoughts were "modified [...] extensively" by Debendranath Tagore, who had a heartfelt way to deal with the improvement of these new principles, addressed focal Hindu convictions like rebirth and karma, and dismissed the power of the Vedas.[53] Tagore additionally brought this "neo-Hinduism" closer by western exclusiveness, an improvement which was facilitated by Sen.[54] Sen was affected by introspective philosophy, an American philosophical-strict development emphatically associated with unitarianism, which underlined individual strict experience over simple thinking and theology.[55] Sen strived for "an open, non-renunciatory, everyman sort of otherworldliness", presenting "lay frameworks of profound practice" which can be viewed as models of the sort of Yoga-practices which Vivekananda promoted in the west.[56]

A similar quest for direct instinct and understanding should be visible in Vivekananda. Not happy with his insight into reasoning, Narendra came to "the inquiry which denoted the genuine start of his scholarly mission for God."[47] He inquired as to whether they had come "up close and personal with God", however, none of their responses fulfilled him.[57][36] At this time, Narendra met Debendranath Tagore (the head of Brahmo Samaj) and inquired as to whether he had seen God. Rather than responding to his inquiry, Tagore said "My kid, you have the Yogi's eyes."[47][41] According to Bhatti, it was Ramakrishna who truly addressed Narendra's inquiry, by saying "OK, I see Him as I see you, just in a vastly intenser sense."[47] According to De Michelis, Vivekananda was more affected by the Brahmo Samaj's and its groundbreaking thoughts, than by Ramakrishna.[56] Swami Medhananda concurs that the Brahmo Samaj was a developmental influence,[58] yet that "it was Narendra's earth-shattering experience with Ramakrishna that steered his life by dismissing him from Brahmoism."[59] According to De Michelis, it was Sen's impact that carried Vivekananda completely into contact with western elusiveness, and it was likewise using Sen that he met Ramakrishna.[60]

In 1881 Narendra initially met Ramakrishna, who turned into his profound concentration after his dad had kicked the bucket in 1884.[61]

Narendra's most memorable prologue to Ramakrishna happened in a writing class at General Assembly's Institution when he heard Professor William Hastie addressing William Wordsworth's sonnet, The Excursion.[51] While making sense of "daze" in the sonnet, Hastie recommended that his understudies visit Ramakrishna of Dakshineswar to grasp the genuine importance of daze. This provoked a portion of his understudies (counting Narendra) to visit Ramakrishna.[62][63][64]

They presumably initially met and by November 1881,[note 1] however Narendra didn't think about this as their most memorable gathering, and neither one of the men referenced this gathering later.[62] At this time, Narendra was planning for his impending F. A. assessment, when Ram Chandra Datta went with him to Surendra Nath Mitra's, home where Ramakrishna was welcome to convey a lecture.[66] According to Makarand Paranjape, at this gathering, Ramakrishna requested that youthful Narendra sing. Dazzled by his singing ability, he requested that Narendra come to Dakshineshwar.[67]

In late 1881 or mid-1882, Narendra went to Dakshineswar with two companions and met Ramakrishna.[62] This gathering ended up being a defining moment in his life.[68] Although he didn't at first acknowledge Ramakrishna as his educator and opposed his thoughts, he was drawn in by his character and started to regularly visit him at Dakshineswar.[69] He at first saw Ramakrishna's euphorias and dreams as "simple fantasies of imagination"[27] and "hallucinations".[70] As an individual from Brahmo Samaj, he went against icon love, polytheism, and Ramakrishna's love of Kali.[71] He even dismissed the Advaita Vedanta of "personality with the outright" as profanation and franticness and frequently derided the idea.[70] Narendra tried Ramakrishna, who confronted his contentions calmly: "Attempt to see reality from all points", he replied.[69]

Narendra's dad's abrupt demise in 1884 remaining the family bankrupt; leasers started requesting the reimbursement of advances, and family members took steps to expel the family from their genealogical home. Narendra, when a child of a wealthy family, became perhaps the most unfortunate understudy in his college.[72] He fruitlessly attempted to look for a job and scrutinized God's existence,[73] yet found comfort in Ramakrishna and his visits to Dakshineswar increased.[74]

At some point, Narendra mentioned Ramakrishna to implore goddess Kali for their family's monetary government assistance. Ramakrishna proposed he go to the sanctuary himself and implore him. Following Ramakrishna's idea, he went to the sanctuary threefold, however, neglected to appeal to God for any sort of common necessities and eventually petitioned God for genuine information and dedication from the goddess.[75][76][77] Narendra continuously developed prepared to deny everything for acknowledging God and acknowledged Ramakrishna as his Guru.[69]

In 1885, Ramakrishna created throat malignant growth and was moved to Calcutta and (later) to a nursery house in Cossipore. Narendra and Ramakrishna's different pupils dealt with him during his last days, and Narendra's otherworldly training proceeded. At Cossipore, he encountered Nirvikalpa samadhi.[78] Narendra and a few different devotees got ochre robes from Ramakrishna, framing his most memorable devout order.[79] He was instructed that assistance to men was the best love of

God.[27][78] Ramakrishna requested that he care for the other religious followers, and thus requested that they see Narendra as their leader.[80] Ramakrishna passed on in the early-morning long stretches of 16 August 1886 in Cossipore.[80][81]

After Ramakrishna's passing, his fans and admirers quit supporting his disciples.[82] An unpaid lease was collected, and Narendra and different followers needed to track down another spot to live.[83] Many got back, embracing a Grihastha (family-situated) method of life.[84] Narendra chose to change over a haggard house at Baranagar into another math (cloister) for the leftover pupils. The lease for the Baranagar Math was low, raised by "blessed asking" (mādhukarī). The math turned into the principal working of the Ramakrishna Math: the cloister of the devout request of Ramakrishna.[68] Narendra and different followers used to spend numerous hours rehearsing contemplation and strict severities each day.[85] Narendra later thought back about the beginning of the monastery:[86]

> "*We went through a great deal of strict practice at the Baranagar Math. We used to get up at 3:00 AM and become retained in Japa and reflection. What a solid soul of separation we had back then! We had no thought even regard to regardless of whether the world existed.*"

In 1887, Narendra ordered a Bengali tune collection named Sangeet Kalpataru with Vaishnav Charan Basak. Narendra gathered and organized a large portion of the tunes of this gathering, yet couldn't completely be crafted by the book for troublesome circumstances.[87]

In December 1886, the mother of Baburam[note 2]

welcomed Narendra and his other sibling priests to Antpur town. Narendra and the other hopeful priests acknowledged the greeting and went to Antpur to put in a couple of days. In Anantapur, on the Christmas Eve of 1886, Narendra and eight different supporters took formal religious vows.[85] They chose to carry on with their lives as their lord lived.[85] Narendranath took the name "Master Vivekananda".[88]

CHAPTER THREE

Voyages of Swami

In 1888, Narendra left the cloister as a Parivrâjaka — the Hindu strict existence of a meandering priest, "without a fixed home, without ties, free and outsiders any place they go".[89] His bottom belongings were a kamandalu (water pot), staff, and his two most loved books: the Bhagavad Gita and The Imitation of Christ.[90] Narendra voyaged widely in India for a considerable length of time, visiting and focused on learning and familiarizing himself with different strict practices and social patterns.[91][92] He created compassion toward the misery and destitution of individuals and set out to elevate the nation.[91][93] Living basically on bhiksha (aid), Narendra walked by railroad (with tickets purchased by admirers). During his movements, he met and remained with Indians from all religions and different backgrounds: researchers, dewans, rajas, Hindus, Muslims, Christians, prayers (low-standing laborers), and government officials.[93] Narendra left Bombay for Chicago on 31 May 1893 with the name "Vivekananda", as recommended by Ajit Singh of Khetri,[94] which signifies "the euphoria of knowing insight," from Sanskrit Viveka and ānanda.[95]

Vivekananda began his excursion toward the West on 31 May 1893[96] and visited a few urban areas in Japan (counting Nagasaki, Kobe, Yokohama, Osaka, Kyoto, and Tokyo),[97] China, and Canada in transit to the United States,[96] arriving at Chicago on 30 July 1893,[98][96] where the "Parliament of Religions" occurred in September 1893.[99] The Congress was a driven by the Swedenborgian layman, and judge of the Illinois Supreme Court, Charles C. Bonney,[100][101] to accumulate every one of the religions of the world, and show "the significant solidarity of numerous religions in the great deeds of the strict life."[100] It was one of the over 200 assistant get-togethers and congresses of the Chicago's World's Fair,[100] and was "a vanguard scholarly appearance of [...] cultic milieus, East and West,"[102] with the Brahmo Samaj and the Theosophical Society being welcomed as being illustrative of Hinduism.[103]

Vivekananda needed to join, yet was disheartened to discover that nobody without certifications from a true blue association would be acknowledged as a delegate.[104] Vivekananda reached Professor John Henry Wright of Harvard University, who welcomed him to talk at Harvard.[104] Vivekananda composed of the teacher, "He encouraged upon me the need of going to the Parliament of Religions, which he thought would give a prologue to the nation".[105][note 3] Vivekananda presented an application, "presenting himself as a priest 'of the most seasoned request of sannyāsis ... established by Sankara,'"[103] upheld by the Brahmo Samaj delegate Protapchandra Mozoombar, who was likewise an individual from the Parliament's determination board, "grouping the Swami as a delegate of the Hindu devout order."[103]

Hearing Vivekananda speak, Harvard brain science teacher William James said, "that man is a miracle for stylistic power. He is a distinction to humanity."[106]
The Parliament of the World's Religions opened on 11 September 1893 at the Art Institute of Chicago, a region of the planet Columbian Exposition.[107][108][109] On this day, Vivekananda gave a concise discourse addressing India and Hinduism.[110] He was at first anxious, bowed to Saraswati (the Hindu goddess of learning), and started his discourse with "Siblings of America!".[111][109] At these words, Vivekananda got two-minute overwhelming applause from the horde of seven thousand.[112] According to Sailendra Nath Dhar, when quiet was reestablished he started his location, welcoming the most youthful of the countries for the benefit of "the eldest request of priests on the planet, the Vedic request of sannyasins, a religion which has shown the world both resistance and widespread acceptance".[113][note 4] Vivekananda cited two illustrative sections from the "Shiva Mahima stotram": "As the various streams having their sources in better places all blend their water in the ocean, thus, O Lord, the various ways what men take, through various propensities, different however they show up, screwy or straight, all lead to Thee!" and "Whosoever comes to Me, through at all structure, I contact him; all men are battling through ways that in the end lead to Me."[116] According to Sailendra Nath Dhar, "it was just a short discourse, yet it voiced the soul of the Parliament."[116][117]

Parliament President John Henry Barrows said, "India, the Mother of religions was addressed by Swami Vivekananda, the Orange-priest who practiced the greatest impact over his auditors".[111] Vivekananda pulled in far and wide consideration in the press, which considered him the "cyclonic priest from India". The New York Critique expressed, "He is a speaker by divine right, and his solid, astute face in its beautiful setting of yellow and orange was not less fascinating than those sincere words, and the rich, rhythmical expression he gave them". The New York Herald noted, "Vivekananda is without a doubt the best figure in the Parliament of Religions. After hearing him we feel that it is so silly to send evangelists to this learned nation".[118] American papers revealed Vivekananda as "the best figure in the parliament of religions" and "the most famous and persuasive man in the parliament".[119] The Boston Evening Transcript detailed that Vivekananda was "an extraordinary number one at the parliament... if he simply crosses the stage, he is applauded".[120] He talked a few additional times "at gatherings, the logical segment, and private homes"[113] on subjects connected with Hinduism, Buddhism, and concordance among religions until the parliament finished on 27 September 1893. Vivekananda's talks at the Parliament had the normal subject of comprehensiveness, underscoring strict tolerance.[121] He before long became known as an "attractive oriental" and established a gigantic connection as an orator.[122]

After the Parliament of Religions, he visited many pieces of the US as a visitor. His fame opened up new perspectives for developing "life and religion to thousands".[122] During an inquiry answer meeting at Brooklyn Ethical Society, he commented, "I have a message toward the West as Buddha had a message toward the East."

Vivekananda went through almost two years addressing the eastern and focal United States, essentially in Chicago, Detroit, Boston, and New York. He established the Vedanta

Society of New York in 1894.[124] By spring 1895 he caught up with, a tiring timetable that had impacted his health.[125] He finished his talk visits and started giving free, confidential classes in Vedanta and yoga. Starting in June 1895, Vivekananda gave private talks to twelve of his supporters at Thousand Island Park, New York for two months.[125]

During his most memorable visit to the West, he ventured out to the UK two times, in 1895 and 1896, addressing effectively there.[126] In November 1895, he met Margaret Elizabeth Noble an Irish lady who might become Sister Nivedita.[125] During his second visit to the UK in May 1896, Vivekananda met Max Müller, a prominent Indologist from Oxford University who composed Ramakrishna's most memorable life story in the West.[117] From the UK, Vivekananda visited other European nations. In Germany, he met Paul Deussen, one more Indologist.[127] Vivekananda was offered scholarly situations in two American colleges (one the seat in Eastern Philosophy at Harvard University and a comparative situation at Columbia University); he declined both since his obligations would struggle with his responsibility as a monk.[125]

Vivekananda's prosperity prompted an adjustment of mission, specifically the foundation of Vedanta focuses on the West.[129] Vivekananda adjusted conventional Hindu thoughts and legalism to suit the requirements and understandings of his western crowds, who were particularly drawn in by and acquainted with western recondite customs and developments like Transcendentalism and New thought.[130] A significant component in his transformation of Hindu legalism was the presentation of his "four yogas" model, which incorporates

Raja yoga, his translation of Patanjali's Yoga sutras,[131] which offered a commonsense means to understand the heavenly power inside which is vital to current western esotericism.[130] In 1896, his book Raja Yoga was distributed, turning into a moment achievement; it was profoundly persuasive in the western comprehension of yoga, in Elizabeth de Michelis' view denoting the start of current yoga.[132][133]

Vivekananda pulled in adherents and admirers in the US and Europe, including Josephine MacLeod, Betty Leggett, Lady Sandwich, William James, Josiah Royce, Robert G. Ingersoll, Lord Kelvin, Harriet Monroe, Ella Wheeler Wilcox, Sarah Bernhardt, Nikola Tesla, Emma Calvé and Hermann Ludwig Ferdinand von Helmholtz.[27][125][127][134][135] He started a few supporters: Marie Louise (a French lady) became Swami Abhayananda, and Leon Landsberg became Swami Kripananda,[136] with the goal that they could proceed with crafted by the mission of the Vedanta Society. This general public is loaded up with outside nationals and is likewise situated in Los Angeles.[137] During his visit to America, Vivekananda was given land in the mountains toward the southeast of San Jose, California to layout a retreat for Vedanta understudies. He referred to it as "Harmony retreat", or, Shanti Asrama.[138] The biggest American community is the Vedanta Society of Southern California in Hollywood, one of the twelve primary places. There is likewise a Vedanta Press in Hollywood which distributes books about Vedanta and English interpretations of Hindu sacred writings and texts.[139] Christina Greenstidel of Detroit was likewise started by Vivekananda with a mantra and she became Sister Christine,[140] and they laid out a nearby dad girl relationship.[141]

From the West, Vivekananda resuscitated his work in India. He routinely related with his devotees and sibling monks,[note 5] contributing guidance and monetary help. His letters from this period mirror his mission of social service,[142] and were unequivocally worded.[143] He kept in touch with Akhandananda, "Go from one way to another among poor people and lower classes of the town of Khetri and show them religion. Additionally, let them have oral illustrations on geology and such different subjects. No decent will happen to sitting inactive and having regal dishes, and saying "Ramakrishna, O Lord!" — except if you can be beneficial to the poor".[144][145] In 1895, Vivekananda established the periodical Brahmavadin to show the Vedanta.[146] Later, Vivekananda's interpretation of the initial six parts of The Imitation of Christ was distributed in Brahmavadin in 1899.[147] Vivekananda left for India on 16 December 1896 from England with his followers Captain and Mrs. Sevier and J.J. Goodwin. On the way, they visited France and Italy and set forth for India from Naples on 30 December 1896.[148] He was subsequently followed to India by Sister Nivedita, who dedicated the remainder of her life to the training of Indian ladies and India's independence.[125][149]

CHAPTER FOUR

Back in India

The boat from Europe showed up in Colombo, British Ceylon (presently Sri Lanka) on 15 January 1897,[148] and Vivekananda got a warm gladly received. In Colombo, he gave his most memorable public discourse in the East. From that point on, his excursion to Calcutta was victorious. Vivekananda went from Colombo to Pamban, Rameswaram, Ramnad, Madurai, Kumbakonam, and Madras, conveying addresses. Average citizens and rajas gave him an exciting gathering. During his train voyages, individuals frequently sat on the rails to drive the train to stop, so they could hear him.[148] From Madras (presently Chennai), he proceeded with his excursion to Calcutta and Almora. While in the West, Vivekananda talked about India's extraordinary profound legacy; in India, he more than once resolved social issues: elevating individuals, disposing of the rank framework, advancing science and industrialization, tending to boundless neediness, and finishing pilgrim rule. These talks, distributed as Lectures from Colombo to Almora, show his nationalistic intensity and profound ideology.[150]

On 1 May 1897 in Calcutta, Vivekananda established the Ramakrishna Mission for social help. Its goals depend on Karma Yoga,[151][152] and its overseeing body comprises the legal administrators of the Ramakrishna Math (which conducts strict work).[153] Both Ramakrishna Math and Ramakrishna Mission have their base camp at Belur Math.[117][154] Vivekananda established two different religious communities: one in Mayavati in the Himalayas (close to Almora), the Advaita Ashrama, and one more in Madras (presently Chennai). Two diaries were established: Prabuddha Bharata in English and Udbhodan in Bengali.[155] That year, starvation alleviation work was started by Swami Akhandananda in the Murshidabad district.[117][153]

Vivekananda prior roused Jamsetji Tata to set up an examination and instructive establishment when they went together from Yokohama to Chicago on Vivekananda's most memorable visit to the West in 1893. Goodbye presently requested that he head his Research Institute of Science; Vivekananda declined the proposition, referring to contention with his "profound interests".[156][157][158] He visited Punjab, endeavoring to intercede in a philosophical struggle between Arya Samaj (a reformist Hindu development) and Sanatan (universal Hindus).[159] After brief visits to Lahore,[153] Delhi, and Khetri, Vivekananda got back to Calcutta in January 1898. He united crafted by the math and prepared followers for a considerable length of time. Vivekananda created "Khandana Bhava-Bandhana", a request melody committed to Ramakrishna, in 1898.[160]

Emerge, conscious, and stop not till the objective is reached, the axiom of Vivekananda was said on 26 January 1897 in Kumbakonam, Tamil Nadu.

Regardless of declining well-being, Vivekananda left for the West briefly time in June 1899[161] joined by Sister Nivedita and Swami Turiyananda. Following a short stay in

England, he went to the United States. During this visit, Vivekananda laid out Vedanta Societies in San Francisco and New York and established a Shanti ashrama (harmony retreat) in California.[162] He then, at that point, went to Paris for the Congress of Religions in 1900.[163] His talks in Paris concerned the love of the lingam and the realness of the Bhagavad Gita.[162] Vivekananda then visited Brittany, Vienna, Istanbul, Athens, and Egypt. The French rationalist Jules Bois was his host for a large portion of this period until he got back to Calcutta on 9 December 1900.[162]

After a short visit to the Advaita Ashrama in Mayavati, Vivekananda settled at Belur Math, where he proceeded with co-ordinating crafted by Ramakrishna Mission, the math and the work in England and the US. He had numerous guests, including sovereignty and government officials. Even though Vivekananda couldn't go to the Congress of Religions in 1901 in Japan due to falling apart wellbeing, he made journeys to Bodhgaya and Varanasi.[164] Declining wellbeing (counting asthma, diabetes, and ongoing sleep deprivation) confined his activity.[165]

CHAPTER FIVE

Nirvana

On 4 July 1902 (the day of his death),[166] Vivekananda stirred early, went to the religious community at Belur Math, and pondered for three hours. He showed Shukla-Yajur-Veda, Sanskrit language structure, and the way of thinking of yoga to pupils,[167][168] later examining with partners an arranged Vedic school in the Ramakrishna Math. At 7:00 PM Vivekananda went to his room, asking not to be disturbed;[167] he kicked the bucket at 9:20 p.m. while meditating.[169] According to his pupils, Vivekananda accomplished mahasamādhi;[170] the burst of a vein in his mind was accounted for as a potential reason for death.[171] His followers accepted that the break was because of his brahmarandhra (an opening in the crown of his head) being penetrated when he achieved mahasamādhi. Vivekananda satisfied his prediction that he wouldn't reside forty years.[172] He was incinerated on a sandalwood memorial service fire on the bank of the Ganga in Belur, inverse where Ramakrishna was incinerated sixteen years earlier.[173]

CHAPTER SIX

Philosophy

While combining and advocating different strands of Hindu thought, most prominently old-style yoga and (Advaita) Vedanta, Vivekananda was impacted by western thoughts like Universalism, using Unitarian ministers who teamed up with the Brahmo Samaj.[6][174][7][175][176] His underlying convictions were molded by Brahmo's ideas, which remembered conviction for an undefined God and the belittling of idolatry,[29][51] and a "smoothed out, legitimized, monotheistic religious philosophy emphatically shaded by a specific and futuristic perusing of the Upanisads and the Vedanta".[177] He proliferated the possibility that "the heavenly, the outright, exists inside all individuals paying little mind to social status",[178] and that "seeing the heavenly as the pith of others will advance love and social harmony".[178] Via his affiliations with Keshub Chandra Sen's Nava Vidhan,[179] the Freemasonry lodge,[180] the Sadharan Brahmo Samaj,[179][34][47][48] and Sen's Band of Hope, Vivekananda got to know Western esotericism.[8]

He was likewise impacted by Ramakrishna, who progressively carried Narendra to a Vedanta-based perspective that "gives the ontological premise to 'śivajñāne jīver sevā', the otherworldly act of serving people as genuine signs of God."[181]

Vivekananda proliferated that the quintessence of Hinduism was best communicated in Adi Shankara's Advaita Vedanta philosophy.[182] Nevertheless, following Ramakrishna, and as opposed to Advaita Vedanta, Vivekananda accepted that the Absolute is both characteristic and transcendent.[note 6] According to Anil Sooklal, Vivekananda's neo-Vedanta "accommodates Dvaita or dualism and Advaita or non-dualism," seeing Brahman as "one without a second," yet "both qualified, sauna, and qualityless, nirguna."[185][note 7] Vivekananda summed up the Vedanta as follows, giving it a cutting edge and Universalistic interpretation,[182] showing the impact of old-style yoga:

Every spirit is possibly heavenly. The objective is to show this Divinity inside by controlling nature, outer and inner. Do this either by work, or love, or mental discipline, or theory — by, at least one, or these — and be free. This is the entire religion. Regulations, authoritative opinions, ceremonies, books, sanctuaries, or structures, are nevertheless auxiliary subtleties.

Vivekananda's accentuation on nirvikalpa samadhi was gone before by middle age yogic impacts on Advaita Vedanta.[186] By Advaita Vedanta texts like Dṛg-Dṛśya-Viveka (fourteenth hundred years) and Vedantasara (of Sadananda) (fifteenth hundred years), Vivekananda saw samadhi as a way to achieve liberation.[187][note 8]

Vivekananda promoted the thought of involution, a term which Vivekananda presumably took from western Theosophists, outstandingly Helena Blavatsky, notwithstanding Darwin's idea of development, and potentially alluding to the Samkhya expression sātkarya.[190] Theosophic thoughts on involution have "much in like manner" with "speculations of the plummet of God in Gnosticism, Kabbalah, and other exclusive schools."[190] According to Meera Nanda, "Vivekananda utilizes the word involution precisely the way that it shows up in Theosophy: the drop, or the contribution, of heavenly consciousness into the matter."[191] With soul, Vivekananda alludes to prana or Purusha, determined ("for certain unique turns") from Samkhya and traditional yoga as introduced by Patanjali in the Yoga sutras.[191]

Vivekananda connected profound quality with control of the psyche, seeing truth, virtue, and unselfishness as characteristics that fortified it.[192] He encouraged his supporters to be blessed, unselfish, and to have shraddhā (confidence). Vivekananda upheld brahmacharya,[193] trusting it as the wellspring of his physical and mental endurance and eloquence.[194]

Vivekananda's colleague with Western elusiveness made him exceptionally fruitful in Western obscure circles, starting with his discourse in 1893 at the Parliament of Religions. Vivekananda adjusted conventional Hindu thoughts and legalism to suit the necessities and understandings of his Western crowds, who were particularly drawn in by and acquainted with Western exclusive customs and developments like Transcendentalism and New thought.[195] A significant component in his transformation of Hindu legalism was the presentation of his four yoga models, which incorporates Raja yoga, his translation of Patanjali's Yoga sutras,[196] which offered a down-to-earth means to understand the heavenly power inside which is key to current Western esotericism.[195] In 1896 his book Raja Yoga was distributed, which turned into a moment achievement and was exceptionally compelling in the Western comprehension of yoga.[197][198]

Patriotism was an unmistakable subject in Vivekananda's thought. He accepted that a country's future relies upon its kin, and his lessons zeroed in on human development.[199] He needed "to get underway a hardware which will carry noblest plans to the doorstep of even the least fortunate and the meanest".[200]

Vivekananda was one of the fundamental delegates of Neo-Vedanta, a cutting edge translation of chosen parts of Hinduism by western recondite practices, particularly Transcendentalism, New Thought and Theosophy.[3] His reevaluation was, and is, exceptionally effective, making another comprehension and enthusiasm for Hinduism inside and outside India,[3] and was the chief justification for the energetic gathering of yoga, Transcendental Meditation, and different types of Indian profound personal development in the West.[201] Agehananda Bharati made sense of, "...modern Hindus determine their insight into Hinduism from Vivekananda, straightforwardly or indirectly".[202] Vivekananda embraced the possibility that all factions inside Hinduism (and all religions) are in various ways to the equivalent goal.[203] However, this view has been reprimanded as a distortion of Hinduism.[203]

Behind the scenes of arising patriotism in British-administered India, Vivekananda solidified the nationalistic ideal. In the expressions of social reformer Charles Freer Andrews, "The Swami's brave positive energy gave another variety to the public development all through India. More than some other single person of that period Vivekananda had made his commitment to the new arousing of India".[204] Vivekananda caused to notice the degree of destitution in the nation, and kept up with that tending to such neediness was essential for public awakening.[205] His nationalistic thoughts impacted numerous Indian masterminds and pioneers. Sri Aurobindo viewed Vivekananda as the person who stirred India spiritually.[206] Mahatma Gandhi considered him as a part of a couple of Hindu reformers "who have kept up with this Hindu religion in a condition of magnificence by chopping down the deadwood of tradition".[207]

In September 2010, the then Union Finance Minister Pranab Mukherjee, the President of India before the ongoing President Ram Nath Kovind, supported on a fundamental level the Swami Vivekananda Values Education Project at an expense of ?1 billion (US$13 million), with goals including: including youth with contests, papers, conversations and review circles and distributing Vivekananda's works in various languages.[208] In 2011, the West Bengal Police Training College was renamed the Swami Vivekananda State Police Academy, West Bengal.[209] The state-specialized college in Chhattisgarh has been named the Chhattisgarh Swami Vivekanand Technical University.[210] In 2012, the Raipur air terminal was renamed Swami Vivekananda Airport.[211]

While National Youth Day in India is seen on his birthday, 12 January, the day he conveyed his mind-blowing discourse at the Parliament of Religions, 11 September 1893, is "World Brotherhood Day".[212][213] The 150th birth commemoration of Swami Vivekananda was praised in India and abroad. The Ministry of Youth Affairs and Sports in India formally noticed 2013 as the event in a declaration.[214]

Indian movie chief Utpal Sinha made a film, The Light: Swami Vivekananda as a recognition of his 150th birth anniversary.[215] Other Indian movies about his life include Swamiji (1949) by Amar Mullick, Swami Vivekananda (1955) by Amar Mullick, Birieswar Vivekananda (1964) by Madhu Bose, Life and Message of Swami Vivekananda (1964) narrative film by Bimal Roy, Swami Vivekananda (1998) by G. V. Iyer, Swamiji (2012) laser light movie by Manick Sorcar.[216] Sound of Joy, an Indian 3D-energized short movie coordinated by Sukankan Roy portrays the otherworldly excursion of Vivekananda. It won the National Film Award for Best Non-Feature Animation Film in 2014.[217]

Even though Vivekananda was a strong speaker and essayist in English and Bengali,[218] he was not an exhaustive scholar,[219] and the greater part of his distributed works was ordered from addresses given all over the planet which were "mostly conveyed [...] extemporaneous and with little preparation".[219] His fundamental work, Raja Yoga, comprises talks he conveyed in New York.[220]

As indicated by Banhatti, "[a] vocalist, a painter, a magnificent expert of language and a writer, Vivekananda was a finished artist",[221] forming numerous tunes and sonnets, including his favorite,[citation needed] "Kali the Mother". Vivekananda mixed humor with his lessons and his language was clear. His Bengali compositions vouch for his conviction that words (verbally expressed or composed) ought to explain thoughts, instead of exhibiting the speaker's (or author's) knowledge.[citation needed]

Bartaman Bharat signifying "Present Day India"[222] is a scholarly Bengali language exposition composed by him, which was first distributed in the March 1899 issue of Udbodhan, the main Bengali language magazine of Ramakrishna Math and Ramakrishna Mission. The paper was republished as a book in 1905 and later gathered into the fourth volume of The Complete Works of Swami Vivekananda.[223] [224]In this exposition his hold back to the perusers was to respect and regard each Indian as a sibling independent of whether he was conceived poor or in a lower caste.[225]

9 798887 171753

Printed by Libri Plureos GmbH in Hamburg,
Germany